HEROES OF WORLD WAR II

The author dedicates this book to his grandfather Roy Keene, born in 1922. He served on the USS *Jicarilla*, an ocean-going tug that was 205 feet long, with a 38-foot beam and 95 crewmembers. Boatswain's Mate, Second Class, Roy and his fellow sailors rode out a typhoon in the South Pacific that capsized three destroyers and drowned nearly 1,000 men. Today Roy lives in Lutz, Florida, with his wife, Margaret. They have four children, thirteen grandchildren, and twenty-four great-grandchildren.

Published by Bushel & Peck Books, a family-run publishing house in Fresno, California, who believes in uplifting children with the highest standards of art, music, literature, and ideas. For every book we sell, we donate one to a child in need—book for book. To nominate a school or organization to receive free books, or to find inspiring books and gifts, please visit www.bushelandpeckbooks.com.

Public-domain period photos, maps, and illustrations sourced through Wikimedia Commons. Other image credits include: Lancaster bombers: Matt Gibson / Shutterstock.com; "We Can Do It!" poster: National Archives (public domain); "Buy War Bonds" poster with Uncle Sam: Everett Collection / Shutterstock.com; "Her America Must Stay Free!" poster: Everett Collection / Shutterstock.com; "WAAC" poster: Everett Collection / Shutterstock.com; "Back Them Up!" poster: Everett Collection / Shutterstock.com; "United We Are Strong, United We Will Win!" poster: Everett Collection / Shutterstock.com; "Smoking Stacks Attract Attacks" poster: Library of Congress (public domain); President Harry Truman portrait: whitehouse.gov (public domain); Andrew Garfield at the "Hacksaw Ridge" Screening: Kathy Hutchins / Shutterstock.com; Urasoe Castle Ruins: Sean Pavone / Shutterstock.com; detail of General Charles de Gaulle: svic / Shutterstock.com; Parisian resistance: Everett Collection / Shutterstock.com; Adolf Hitler circa 1930s: murathakanart / Shutterstock.com; Biuki Gassa: JFK Presidential Library and Museum; letter excerpt about John F. Kennedy's rescuer: JFK Presidential Library and Museum; vintage film background: STILLFX / Shutterstock.com; USS Arizona Memorial: Daniel De Petro / Shutterstock.com; Lavockine La-5: Newresid via Wikimedia Commons; Oskar Schindler's office: agsaz / Shutterstock.com; Jews rescued by Oskar Schindler: meunierd / Shutterstock.com.

LCCN: 2023950345
ISBN: 978-1-63819-171-1

First Edition

Printed in China

1 3 5 7 9 10 8 6 4 2

BUSHEL & PECK'S HEROES REMEMBERED LIBRARY

Jarret Keene

ILLUSTRATED BY
Ricardo Gualberto

25 TRUE STORIES OF UNSUNG HEROES WHO FOUGHT FOR FREEDOM

BUSHEL
& PECK
BOOKS

1
2
3
4
5
6
7
8
9
10
11
12
13
14
15
16
17
18
19
20
21
22
23
24
25

CONTENTS

PEOPLE AND STORIES

UNITED

AUTHOR'S NOTE

Of all the noteworthy military conflicts in history, World War II is perhaps the most challenging to fully capture. There were so many countries involved, so many battles raging across the planet, and so many lives lost, that documenting the story can be upsetting for readers—and for the author. Fortunately, WWII was also a moment when true heroes emerged from the chaos and violence. The book you hold in your hands is only a small collection of tales featuring brave, selfless souls who stood together—and sometimes alone—against an evil empire. While I have made every effort to present the information with utmost care and sensitivity, the savagery of war and the horror of the Holocaust are impossible to avoid. Death can't be glossed over or pictured rosily. I hope that when readers engage this book, they do so with the understanding that wars like the one chronicled here are always close at hand. All it takes is one unhinged world leader, one diabolical national figure, to plunge the globe into relentless, unspeakable bloodshed. We must strive to strengthen and heal our communities in preparation for the possibility of disaster. The best way to do that is to read and understand history, and to listen to different perspectives that surround important, even incendiary issues. Knowledge is of utmost value in difficult times. We must keep in mind Spanish and American philosopher George Santayana's famous maxim: "Those who cannot remember the past are condemned to repeat it." With any luck, this book will stand as a reminder. Keep it close to you when things seem darkest. Remember that heroes still walk the earth today just as they did in years past. Maybe you, or the person sitting next to you in class, is a hero of the future. Stay strong, love your friends and family, and, as British WWII leader Winston Churchill is said to have announced: "Never give in!"

—Jarret Keene

INTRODUCTION

WHAT IS A NAZI?

From 1933 to 1945, Germany was controlled by the National Socialist German Workers' Party. This political movement was sparked by extreme nationalism, racism, and populism. "Nazi" abbreviates the National Socialist party's name, Nationalsozialist.

To fully appreciate the people and events in this book, it's helpful to have some background about what caused World War II, and how nations aligned with and against one another.

HOW WORLD WAR II HAPPENED

The First World War (1914–18) caused so much volatility that another, greater conflict was inevitable. That's exactly what happened 20 years later when Adolf Hitler rose to power. Leader of the Nazi political party and chancellor of Germany, Hitler ignored the treaty that his country signed in 1919. Once again, the German nation and its people prepared for war. With world domination on his mind, Hitler signed treaties with Italy and Japan. He was eager to use these nations to realize his dream of carving out a large space in Europe for Germans and Germany. He also wanted to eradicate the Jews from Europe.

In 1939, the Nazis invaded Poland, an ally of Britain and France. These countries declared war on Germany. World War II, a conflagration unlike any previous military clash, threatened to engulf the planet. Luckily the Allies prevailed in the end.

TREATY OF VERSAILLES

On June 28, 1919, a peace treaty was signed, ending the war between Germany and Allied powers. Germany wasn't permitted to join the negotiations, and its leaders had no choice but to sign it. The nation had to accept guilt and responsibility for losses suffered by the Allies during the conflict. More controversially, Germany had to disarm, surrender territory, and pay reparations in the amount of 132 billion gold marks.

The German people suffered and weren't happy. The atmosphere was ripe for someone like Hitler to come along and demand—or seize—a better deal.

AXIS POWERS

German, Italy, and Japan formed the core group of nations that opposed the Allies. They were joined by Hungary, Romania, Bulgaria, Slovakia, and Croatia.

ALLIED POWERS

After Poland fell to the Nazis, Britain and France stood as the primary Allied powers. They were joined by the United States, the Soviet Union, and China. Allied nations that were overrun by Nazis: Poland, Czechoslovakia, Norway, Netherlands, Belgium, France, Luxembourg, Ethiopia, Greece, Yugoslavia, and the Philippines. Allied nations that joined the fight: India, Canada, Australia, New Zealand, South Africa, Southern Rhodesia, Brazil, Mongolia, and Mexico.

THE HOLOCAUST

Also known in Hebrew as the Shoah (the catastrophe), the Holocaust was the systematic mass killing of 6 million Jews across German-occupied Europe. This was roughly two-thirds of the Jewish population in Europe. The killing was done in many ways: forced death marches, violent riots, shootings, and gas chambers in concentration camps.

U.S. INTERNMENT CAMPS

After the Japanese attack on Pearl Harbor on December 7, 1941, President Franklin D. Roosevelt signed an executive order. It authorized the military to relocate Japanese-American residents to prevent sabotage and espionage. There was never a shred of evidence that Japanese-Americans on the West Coast were planning to destroy or spy on U.S. military facilities. Still, California, Oregon, and the state of Washington required Japanese-Americans to leave their homes, give up their jobs, and live in internment camps. More than 110,000 people suffered from this unjust order. Eventually, the U.S. Supreme Court ruled that detention without cause is unconstitutional in 1944.

THE MANHATTAN PROJECT

The effort to create the first atomic weapon was first conceived in Manhattan, New York. But the bulk of the work was done in the desert facilities of Los Alamos, New Mexico. It took three years (1942–45) to create the device under the leadership of Major General Leslie Groves (U.S. Army Corps of Engineers) and nuclear physicist Robert Oppenheimer.

ITALIAN-AMERICANS DETAINED

In 1942, there were 695,000 Italian immigrants in the United States. Of these, around 1,890 were taken into custody and detained during WWII.

UNITED STATES DEPARTMENT OF JUSTICE

★

NOTICE TO ALIENS OF ENEMY NATIONALITIES

★ The United States Government requires all aliens of German, Italian, or Japanese nationality to apply at post offices nearest to their place of residence for a Certificate of Identification. Applications must be filed between the period February 9 through February 28, 1942. *Go to your postmaster today for printed directions.*

EARL G. HARRISON, Special Assistant to the Attorney General

FRANCIS BIDDLE, Attorney General

AVVISO

Il Governo degli Stati Uniti ordina a tutti gli stranieri di nazionalità Tedesca, Italiana e Giapponese di fare richiesta all' Ufficio Postale più prossimo al loro luogo di residenza per ottenere un Certificato d'Identità. Le richieste devono essere fatte entro il periodo che decorre tra il 9 Febbraio e il 28 Febbraio, 1942.

Andate oggi dal vostro Capo d'Ufficio Postale (Postmaster) per ricevere le istruzioni scritte.

BEKANNTMACHUNG

Die Regierung der Vereinigten Staaten von Amerika fordert alle Auslaender deutscher, italienischer und japanischer Staatsangehoerigkeit auf, sich auf das ihrem Wohnorte naheliegende Postamt zu begeben, um einen Personalausweis zu beantragen. Das Gesuch muss zwischen dem 9. und 28. Februar 1942 eingereicht werden.

Gehen Sie noch heute zu Ihrem Postmeister und verschaffen Sie sich die gedruckten Vorschriften.

敵國外人注意

GERMAN-AMERICANS RELOCATED

During WWII, more than 11,500 people of German ancestry were interned during the war, too. This number comprised 36 percent of total internments under the U.S. Justice Department's Enemy Alien Control Program.

EB. 15 TO FEB. 28

A TIMELINE OF WORLD WAR II

SEPTEMBER 1, 1939
The conflict explodes when the Nazis invade Poland. This action stirs the country's allies, Britain and France, to declare war on Germany.

SEPTEMBER 17
The Soviet Union invades Poland, with Hitler's permission, to claim its own piece of the country.

APRIL 18, 1940
Nazis invade Norway, a country that had remained neutral during the First World War.

MAY 10, 1940
Nazis invade Belgium. The Belgian Army fought bravely, but was defeated in just 18 days.

JUNE 14, 1940
Paris falls to Nazi forces in just 11 days.

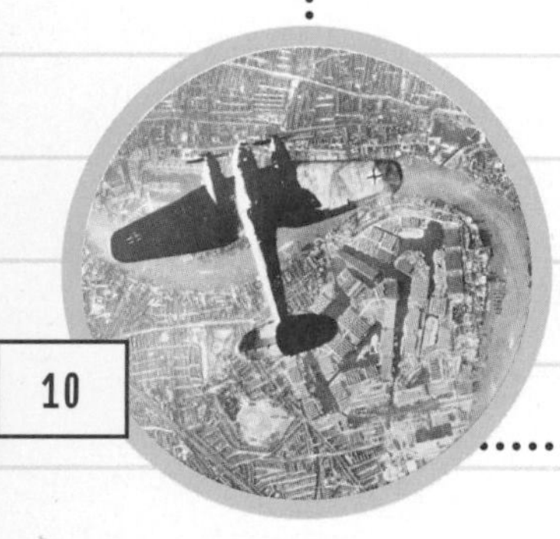

JULY 10-OCTOBER 31, 1940
In the Battle of Britain, Royal Air Force fighters manage a defensive victory even as Nazi bombers reduce London to rubble.

APRIL 6, 1941
Italy, Bulgaria, Hungary, and Germany invade the countries of Greece and Yugoslavia.

JUNE 22, 1941
Hitler invades the Soviet Union in a mobilization called Operation Barbarossa.

DECEMBER 7, 1941
The Empire of Japan bombs Pearl Harbor, bringing the United States into the conflict. Hitler declares war on America a week later.

JUNE 4-7, 1942
The Battle of Midway is a major air-and-sea victory for the U.S. Navy against Japan. America successfully defends its base at Midway Island, ruins Japan's hopes of demolishing the United States as a naval power, and turns the tide of WWII in the Pacific theater.

AUGUST 23, 1942-FEBRUARY 2, 1943
The Axis ultimately fails in wrestling away Stalingrad, a city in Southern Russia, from the Soviets.

ACK THEM UP!

NOVEMBER 8-16, 1942
Operation Torch: Allied forces storm North Africa in a ploy to draw Axis forces away from the Eastern Front.

MAY 12, 1943
Axis forces (the German-Italian army) surrender in North Africa. Campaigns were fought in Libya, Egypt, Morocco, Algeria (Operation Torch), and Tunisia.

AUGUST 17, 1943
The Allies take over Sicily after a large amphibious and airborne operation, and then a six-week land campaign. This victory launches the Italian campaign.

SEPTEMBER 3, 1943
Italy surrenders, but the war is far from over.

JANUARY 27, 1944
The Nazis give up on trying to take Leningrad and retreat.

JUNE 6, 1944
D-Day in Normandy, France, is launched, kicking off the liberation of France and providing the groundwork for Allied victory on the Western Front.

AUGUST 25, 1944
Paris is liberated by Allied forces. Nazis continue to retreat.

DECEMBER 16, 1944-JANUARY 25, 1945
The Battle of the Bulge, also called the Ardennes Offensive, is the last major German campaign on the Western Front during WWII. From here on, the Nazis are in full retreat.

APRIL 12, 1945
U.S. President Franklin D. Roosevelt dies at age 63. Vice President Harry S. Truman assumes the presidency.

MAY 2, 1945
The Red Army smashes into Berlin and captures the city. The Third Reich is defeated, and the war ends in Europe.

JULY 25, 1945
President Truman writes in his diary: "We have discovered the most terrible bomb in the history of the world. It may be the fire destruction prophesied in the Euphrates Valley Era, after Noah and his fabulous Ark."

AUGUST 6, 1945
The United States drops an atomic bomb on the Japanese city of Hiroshima.

AUGUST 14, 1945
Japan surrenders, and the Pacific theater of WWII comes to end.

VOLCANIC ISLAND

Located 750 miles from Japan's coast, Iwo Jima is part of a stretch of volcano islands. In the battle, 22,000 Japanese soldiers died. The United States took heavy casualties, too, with 6,800 lives lost.

TWO FLAG-RAISINGS

Ira participated in the second flag-raising. Earlier in the day, different Marines had hoisted a smaller flag. Because it wasn't clearly visible, Ira's colonel ordered Ira and others to raise a larger stars and stripes.

1 IRA HAYES

BORN: 1923, SACATON, ARIZONA
DIED: 1955, BAPCHULE, ARIZONA

It's among the most famous images in American history: six United States Marines raise the U.S. flag atop Mount Suribachi during the Battle of Iwo Jima. One warrior in this dramatic 1945 photo is Ira Hayes (pictured far left), a Pima Indian from the Gila River Reservation in Arizona. Ira was 22 years old at the time, a quiet young man. He would go on to become a legend, a film star, and the subject of a folk song.

An intelligent, patriotic child, Ira grew up shy and sensitive. He learned to read and write by age four. After graduating from Phoenix Indian School in Arizona, he worked as a carpenter. When the Japanese attacked Pearl Harbor, Ira told friends he wanted to join the U.S. Marine Corps.

Within a year, he enlisted. Ira completed paratrooper training at Camp Gillespie (now Gillespie Field) in San Diego, the first Pima Indian to receive silver "jump wings" (parachutist badge). His codename? "Chief Flying Cloud."

He was shipped to the South Pacific to fight in a series of battles between Allied forces and the Empire of Japan. After the Allies triumphed, he landed at Iwo Jima. Ira and his fellow Marines fought their way to the slope of a mountain, ascended the rim, and raised the flag on February 23, 1945. A combat photographer captured the moment. Two days later, thousands of newspapers printed the image, titled *Raising the Flag on Iwo Jima.*

Ira continued to fight at Iwo Jima until March 26. After being shipped to Washington D.C. for promotional war-bond appearances (the photo had made him a celebrity), he was promoted to corporal and awarded commendations and medals. Honorably discharged at war's end, he went on to star as himself alongside Hollywood actor John Wayne in the 1949 film *Sands of Iwo Jima.* In 1964, country-music icon Johnny Cash recorded a song called "The Ballad of Ira Hayes."

Ira never got to hear it. He died young, age 32, from cold exposure in his hometown, but his valiant spirit endures. Ira is buried at Arlington National Cemetery.

THE PHOTOGRAPHER

Associated Press photographer Joe Rosenthal (pictured above) won the Pulitzer Prize, the highest honor in journalism, for *Raising the Flag on Iwo Jima.* Three of the Marines in the photo, however, died in the battle.

AIRFIELD
NO. 2
382
TACH

OSKAR EXPLAINS

In an interview, Oskar (shown above) famously stated: "I hated the brutality, the sadism, and the insanity of Nazism. I just couldn't stand by and see people destroyed. I did what I could, what I had to do, what my conscience told me I must do."

SCHINDLERJUDEN

The Jews Oskar saved came to be known as Schindlerjuden, translated from German as "Schindler's Jews." When Oskar was wanted for war crimes due to his earlier spying, they protected him from prosecution and helped him relocate to Argentina. Eventually he returned to Germany. To the left is what remains of one of Oskar's factories.

2

OSKAR SCHINDLER

BORN: 1908, ZWITTAU, AUSTRIA-HUNGARY
DIED: 1974, HILDESHEIM, GERMANY

A Nazi party member, an aggressive businessman, and a lover of luxury, he is an unlikely hero. Yet Oskar Schindler succeeded in saving more than 1,000 Jews from the death camps.

When the Nazis conquered Poland, Schindler, who had been working as a spy for German intelligence, moved to Krakow. There he operated factories previously owned by Polish Jews. In one factory, called Emalia, he found a way to put Jews to work. They were forced laborers from a nearby concentration camp. Oskar protected them from liquidation by letting them stay overnight in the factory.

Oskar found ways to make Jewish laborers useful and avoid execution. He convinced the Nazis to let him convert part of Emalia into a weapons-making facility. He persuaded the Nazis to let him call Emalia a concentration camp despite the factory work going on. It was risky, people suspected he was up to something, and he was arrested by SS officers and Gestapo agents. But the charges never stuck.

Then the Nazis tried to transfer Emalia-based Jews back to the concentration camp. However, Oskar convinced authorities to let him open a new munitions plant in another town. He swayed them with bogus production estimates and presented a real list of Jewish workers needed to get the plant operational. The list, which included 800 men and 400 women, has come to be known as "Schindler's List." Because the Nazis needed every German to fight the Allies, Oskar kept his workers safe from harm until the end of the war. With little oversight, his factory produced a single truckload of ammunition in eight full months.

For decades, history obscured his rescue. Oskar died alone and penniless in Germany. The people he rescued, however, had him buried in Israel. His name resurfaced, and his efforts became the subject of the historical novel *Schindler's List*, which was adapted into an Academy Award–winning film.

A MUSEUM TO REMEMBER

Schindler's tin metal factory in Krakow, Poland, was turned into a museum in 2010. The permanent exhibition there details the history of the city and its Polish and Jewish residents during WWII. The museum features collections of newspapers, personal documents, and factory artifacts. Oskar's original office is depicted above. Below are some of the Jews rescued by Oskar's efforts.

MOVIE MAGIC

Directed by Mel Gibson and starring Andrew Garfield (above), *Hacksaw Ridge* is the 2016 biographical film based on Desmond's combat experience. The movie won two Oscars and was hailed as the best war movie since *Saving Private Ryan.*

TRUMAN'S OWN WORDS

President Harry S. Truman held Desmond's hand as his Medal of Honor citation was read aloud to everyone gathered outside the White House in October 1945. "I consider this a greater honor than being president," Truman said to the pacifist-hero medic. To the left, Truman pins the Medal of Honor on Desmond's uniform.

3 DESMOND DOSS

BORN: 1919, LYNCHBURG, VIRGINIA
DIED: 2006, PIEDMONT, ALABAMA

He didn't kill a single enemy soldier. He didn't carry a gun. He didn't eat meat. Yet army corporal and combat medic Desmond Doss, with just a Bible and his faith as armor, earned the Congressional Medal of Honor. He also received two Bronze Stars for bravery under fire. How is this possible?

It all goes back to Desmond's upbringing. He was raised in the Seventh-day Adventist Church, an evangelical Christian denomination that stresses health and pacifism. He was working in a Virginia shipyard when he heard about Pearl Harbor. He was offered a deferment that would have kept him building naval vessels. Instead he enlisted in the army. He assumed that declaring himself a conscientious objector would allow him to avoid using weapons. He was wrong.

Commanding officers refused to honor his objector status. They mocked him, intimidated him, and assigned him extra, grueling duties. They tried to court-martial him and declare him mentally unfit. But he didn't break and he didn't bend. Desmond found ways to be useful, treating his fellow soldiers' marching blisters and saving them from dehydration with water from his canteen. He served as a medic in Guam, the Philippines, and in the Battle of Okinawa, coming to the aid of wounded soldiers. The cry would ring out: "Medic!" Desmond would run a gauntlet of whizzing bullets to reach a wounded soldier and carry him to safety. He didn't worry about his own life, only the lives of others. He himself was wounded four times in Okinawa.

In an attempt to punt an enemy grenade away from his combat team, he suffered more than a dozen pieces of shrapnel in his leg. He was sniper-shot in the arm. He contracted tuberculosis, making his later years difficult. He lost a lung and several ribs due to the illness. But Desmond succeeded in raising a family on a small farm and was immortalized in a documentary film and a big-budget Hollywood movie.

LOCATION IS EVERYTHING

Okinawa is an island located on the southwestern tip of the Japanese archipelago. Okinawa's Maeda Escarpment, also known as Hacksaw Ridge, is located atop a 400-foot cliff. Today (shown above), it is a peaceful place of contemplation.

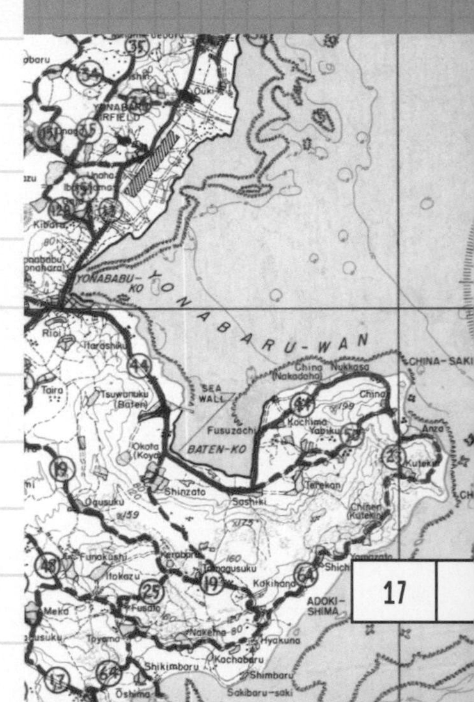

PTSD

Dorothy suffered post-traumatic stress disorder from her imprisonment. However, the U.S. Department of Veterans Affairs dismissed her health concerns. For years, the psychiatric community believed that only combat personnel suffered PTSD.

ANGELS OF BATAAN

These were members of the U.S. Army Nurse Corps and Navy Nurse Corps stationed in the Philippines during the Pacific War. While serving in the Battle of the Philippines (1941–42), 78 nurses were captured and imprisoned by the Japanese. Some of them are pictured on the left.

4

DOROTHY STILL

BORN: 1914, SAGINA, MICHIGAN
DIED: 2001, BOISE, IDAHO

An American Navy nurse is a role that usually involves caring for the wounded in hospitals. At worst, a nurse treats patients in a church or battlefield tent. Dorothy Still tended to the sick and dying in the most wretched conditions imaginable: a prison camp.

For three years, Dorothy was a prisoner of war in the Philippines. With little food and fewer medical supplies, she and other imprisoned nurses constructed a makeshift infirmary with 25 beds. They subsisted on 500 calories a day. They made and washed their own uniforms and medical gowns to keep military and professional bearing in the face of guards and to ensure sanitary conditions. Under constant threat, including execution by machine gun, Dorothy treated thousands of prisoners.

As the Allies battled their way into the island, Dorothy realized her prison camp was not in the line of advance. A rescue would require a special, perhaps unlikely, mission. Dorothy never lost hope, even when guards swore to kill all POWs before they could be liberated. She continued to care for others.

When Dorothy saw aircraft flying, American paratroopers parachuting from the sky, and an amphibious landing vehicle breaking through the fence and driving right up to the prison infirmary, she was elated. She reportedly said about the moment, "Oh, we never saw anything so handsome in our lives."

A historical plaque, displayed in Cavite City in the Philippines, bears Dorothy's name. It lists her as one of the Angels of Bataan.

DEATH MARCH

After the Battle of Bataan in 1942, wounded personnel became Japanese prisoners. They and more than 60,000 Filipinos were forced to march inland for 65 miles and put in prison camps. Historians call this event the "Bataan Death March," pictured above. As many as 500 Americans and 2,500 Filipino soldiers died on the trek.

DE GAULLE'S WARNING

In the run-up to the Fall of France, General Charles de Gaulle (above) urged the French military to invest in mechanized warfare, especially tanks. His plea was ignored. After bravely counteracting the Nazi invasion, he fled to England to cheer the French rejection of Nazism and to lead the Free France movement in exile. He returned to his country as a liberator in 1944.

FRENCH RESISTANCE

After the Nazis took over France, the Resistance formed, uniting people from all parts of French society: émigrés, professors, priests, Protestants, Jews, anarchists, and communists. Two such fighters are pictured on the left. It is estimated that the Resistance comprised a half million people. Of these, 90,000 were captured or killed. The Resistance helped Allied forces advance through France after the Normandy Invasion in 1944.

5 GENEVIÈVE DE GAULLE

BORN: 1920, SAINT-JEAN-DE-VALÉRISCLE, FRANCE
DIED: 2002, PARIS, FRANCE

The French Resistance succeeded because of the brave young women in its ranks—women like 19-year-old Geneviève de Gaulle. Niece of French general and statesman Charles de Gaulle, Geneviève was a young history major in college when the Nazis steamrolled into her country in 1940. She felt she had no choice but to fight back with guerrilla-warfare tactics and by circulating an underground newspaper.

Initially her acts of defiance were small. She started by ripping down posters of Hitler and flags with swastikas. Then she smuggled guns and provided forged travel papers to resistance fighters. Then Geneviève began editing the newspaper *Défense de La France*, the biggest clandestine voice opposing Nazi occupation. Producing the paper made her a target.

Betrayed by French traitors, Geneviève was apprehended by the Gestapo in 1943. She was shipped to the notorious Ravensbrück concentration camp in Berlin, Germany. There the guards nicknamed her "miniature de Gaulle," singling her out for abuse because of her famous uncle. She saw horrifying things: medical experiments and the poison-gassing of Jews. She was put in solitary confinement by Heinrich Himmler, chief of German police. He hoped to one day use her for a prisoner swap.

It never happened. Himmler was captured by the Allies, and he died by swallowing a cyanide pill he'd hidden on his person. But Geneviève survived her imprisonment and went on to launch a nonprofit dedicated to reducing poverty around the world. She wrote a memoir about her wartime experiences and married a fellow resistance member. They had four children.

WHAT'S A SWASTIKA?

The swastika is an ancient religious symbol that the Nazis used for their own purposes. In his manifesto *Mein Kampf* ("My Struggle"), German dictator Adolf Hitler (above) claims to have designed the Nazi emblem: a black swastika rotated 45 degrees against a white circle on a red background. Today it is the universal symbol of hatred and intolerance. Its display is banned many countries.

NUREMBERG TRIALS

From 1945 to 1946, the Allies prosecuted and put on trial representatives of the Nazi regime for their acts of genocide and evil, which were in violation of international law. At the trial's conclusion, ten prominent Nazi leaders were sentenced to death and executed by hanging. Above, several German doctors from concentration camps are put on trial for their crimes.

GAS CHAMBERS

Charles took note of where the gas chambers were located at Monowitz. The Nazis used poison gas to kill 6,000 victims a day at Auschwitz during WWII. On the left, an aerial photo identifies the buildings of the main camp.

6

CHARLES JOSEPH COWARD

BORN: 1905, ENGLAND, UNITED KINGDOM
DIED: 1976, LONDON, ENGLAND

The Allied forces performed many acts of bravery during WWII. But few deeds compare with donning prison clothes and breaking into the Monowitz concentration camp in occupied Poland. This is what British Army sergeant Charles Joseph Coward did while working as a Red Cross liaison officer to British prisoners. This role gave him freedom to move from camp to camp, including the notorious Auschwitz. But the reason he was attempting to make contact with an imprisoned doctor? He had received a note that Monowitz secretly held more British prisoners.

Charles was known by the Allies as a master of breach and escape. He was an unrivaled saboteur against the Nazis, plaguing them during prison work detail. His captors could never seem to hold Charles for long. But this particular feat of stealth was something else entirely.

His mission to find the doctor failed. Later, he testified about what he saw at the camp during the Nuremberg war crimes trials. Charles smuggled 400 prisoners out of the death camps, too. His scheme involved giving clothes and documents of non-Jewish corpses to Jews. This allowed them a chance to adopt false identities, leave the camps, and escape. For this and other exploits, he was dubbed "The Count of Auschwitz."

Charles continued to spy inside the camps until being liberated by the Allies in Bavaria in 1945.

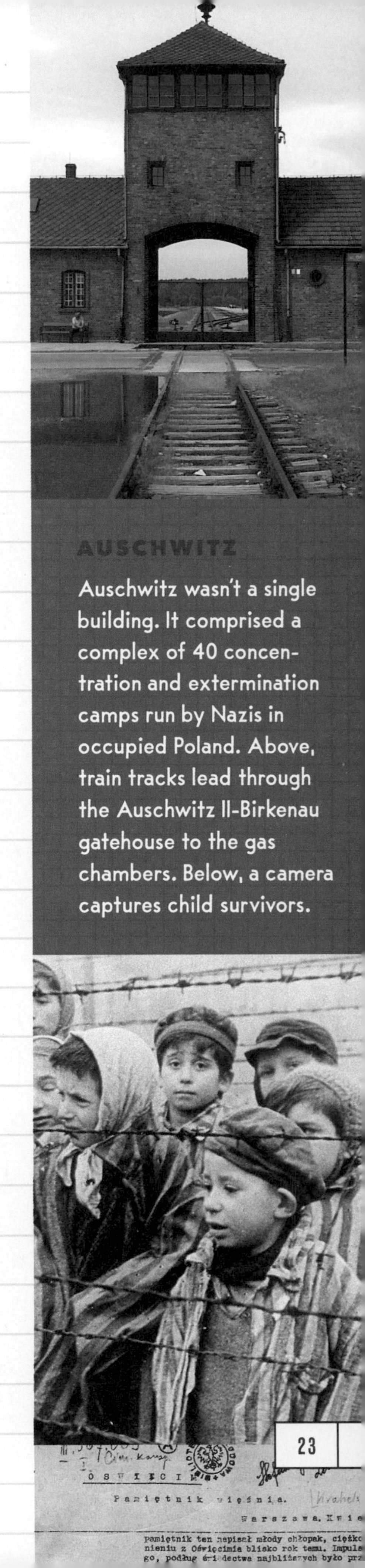

AUSCHWITZ

Auschwitz wasn't a single building. It comprised a complex of 40 concentration and extermination camps run by Nazis in occupied Poland. Above, train tracks lead through the Auschwitz II-Birkenau gatehouse to the gas chambers. Below, a camera captures child survivors.

FLYING THE FIRST LADY

"Well, you can fly all right," announced First Lady Eleanor Roosevelt (shown above in the plane) to reporters in March of 1941. She had just landed after being flown in the air for 30 minutes in a Piper J-3 Cub by Black chief civilian instructor C. Alfred Anderson. A pilot since 1929, Anderson trained pilots in preparation for air combat against the Luftwaffe.

RED TAILS

Tuskegee pilots flew P-51 Mustangs to guard bombers on missions into enemy territory. For identification, the Mustangs' tails were painted red. This earned them the nickname "Red Tails." The plane on the left is a fully restored P-51 Mustang that still flies today!

7 TUSKEGEE AIRMEN

There was strict racial segregation in the U.S. military during WWII. Nonetheless, the United States Army Air Force (USAAF) unleashed the Tuskegee Airmen. This was a group of Black military pilots that trained in Tuskegee, a city in Macon County, Alabama, forming the 332d Fighter Group and the 477th Bombardment Group. The name "Tuskegee Airmen" also encompasses navigators, mechanics, instructors, nurses, cooks, and other support personnel.

The fighter group shot down three German jets in a day while escorting B-17 bombers into Germany and back. The target: a Berlin tank factory defended by the Luftwaffe, the German Air Force. The 332nd Fighter Group earned a Distinguished Unit Citation for this mission. Overall, their missions took them to Italy and Nazi-held areas of central and southern Europe. Fighter pilots flew everything from Curtiss P-40 Warhawks to Bell P-39 Airacobras, from Republic P-47 Thunderbolts to North American P-51 Mustangs.

Overall, the Tuskegee Airmen were highly successful:

- 1,578 combat missions
- 179 bomber escort missions, with a good protection record, losing bombers on only seven missions
- 112 enemy aircraft shot down

The U.S. military was desegregated in 1948 thanks to President Harry S. Truman. He did this by signing an executive order, which resulted in the Committee on Equality of Treatment and Opportunity in the Armed Services.

DEATH IN THE SKIES

In WWII, 355 Black pilots (like the one pictured above) from Tuskegee were deployed into combat: 84 were killed (with a dozen dying in noncombat missions) and 32 captured after their planes were shot down.

BIUKU GASA

One of the highlights in the JFK Presidential Library and Museum is a handwritten note from 1957 (pictured on facing page, bottom right). In it, John pays tribute to Biuku, a Solomon Islander who helped rescue him and his crew. "I don't remember his name," writes John. "I never knew it, but I will never forget him." Biuku, photographed above, died in 2005.

WHERE IS IT?

The JFK Presidential Library and Museum finished construction in Boston, Massachusetts, in 1979. Its "JFK in WWII" exhibit includes his dog tags, naval dress uniform, and scrapbook of wartime photos he took himself. In the photo to the left, John is the man furthest on the right.

8

JOHN F. KENNEDY

BORN: 1917, BROOKLINE, MASSACHUSSETTS
DIED: 1963, DALLAS, TEXAS

He wasn't just the 35th president of the United States. He was also a decorated war hero, earning the Navy and Marine Corps Medal and a Purple Heart for his valiant action in the Pacific theater. He declined the offer of the Bronze Star. Indeed, John F. Kennedy lived the words he famously spoke at his inaugural presidential address: "Ask not what your country can do for you—ask what you can do for your country."

John was 22 years old when he joined the U.S. Navy Reserve in 1941, just prior to the attack on Pearl Harbor. A commissioned officer, he grew bored of life behind a desk. A few years into the war, he volunteered to command a patrol torpedo craft—or PT boat, used to spot enemy submarines. He ended up in the Solomon Islands in the South Pacific.

He was on a mission. The night was pitch-dark, moonless. Suddenly a Japanese destroyer rammed his vessel, breaking it in half and instantly killing two of his crew. Floating in life jackets, John and 10 surviving shipmates decided to swim to an island four miles away. Surrender wasn't an option; fighting without weapons was impossible. So they went for it, John using his teeth to clench the preserver strap of an injured crewman. He swam them to safety.

After reaching the island, they were helped by two Solomon Islanders, Biuku Gasa and Eroni Kumana. John carved a message into a coconut and Biuku and Eroni delivered it to a nearby Allied base. John and his crew were rescued.

Months later, John intentionally put his PT boat between enemy guns and scrambling Marines, shielding them from bullets. John was a hero twice over.

After the war, he was elected to the House of Representatives and then the Senate, representing his home state of Massachusetts. In 1960, he became president. He died, tragically, from an assassin's bullet in 1963 at age 46.

PT BOAT

These were used by the U.S. Navy during WWII to conduct oceanic scouting and to harass enemy supply lines. Below, John is photographed sitting in his PT boat.

DOGFIGHT

A dogfight is an aerial clash between aircraft at close range. Dogfighting was a big part of every war until the early 1990s, when high-tech missiles made such aerial combat maneuvering obsolete. Above, sailors observe the contrails from planes dogfighting during World War II's Battle of the Philippine Sea.

ZERO

The Mitsubishi A6M "Zero" (left) was a long-range carrier-based fighter aircraft operated by the Imperial Japanese Navy from 1940 to 1945. The Zero's superb design made it highly maneuverable, which was ideal for dogfighting.

JOE FOSS

BORN: 1915, SIOUX FALLS, SOUTH DAKOTA
DIED: 2003, SCOTTSDALE, ARIZONA

He aspired to be a fighter pilot, but he was 27 years old—an old man in air-combat years. So Joe learned to be an aerial photographer. Still, he never completely gave up on his dream. Finally his request to join a fighter-pilot qualification program was honored. He was assigned to a training squadron to fly the Grumman F4F Wildcat. After spending 150 hours in the air, he joined a Marine fighter squadron. He entered the Pacific theater in October 1942 and fought in the Battle of Guadalcanal.

He shot down a Japanese Zero on his very first mission. However, his Wildcat took damage. He was forced to crash-land into a grove of palm trees. But his reputation was established: He had a knack for close-up, aggressive gunnery skills. In the months that followed, he shot down 26 enemy fighters. Joe was named the first "Ace of Aces" of WWII and is listed as being among the best fighter pilots of the 20th century. He earned the Congressional Medal of Honor for his aerial victories.

When the war ended, Joe was appointed a lieutenant colonel in the South Dakota Air National Guard. When the Korean War kicked off, Joe was promoted from colonel to the rank of brigadier general. He was elected the youngest governor (at age 39) of South Dakota in 1955. He went on to serve as the first commissioner of the American Football League and as the president of the National Rifle Association.

KAMIKAZE

These Japanese pilots flew suicide attacks against the Allies near the end of the Pacific campaign of WWII with the intent of destroying warships. It is estimated that 3,800 kamikaze pilots died during the war, with 7,000 Allied personnel killed by kamikaze attacks. Above, the USS *Bunker Hill* is hit by two kamikazes.

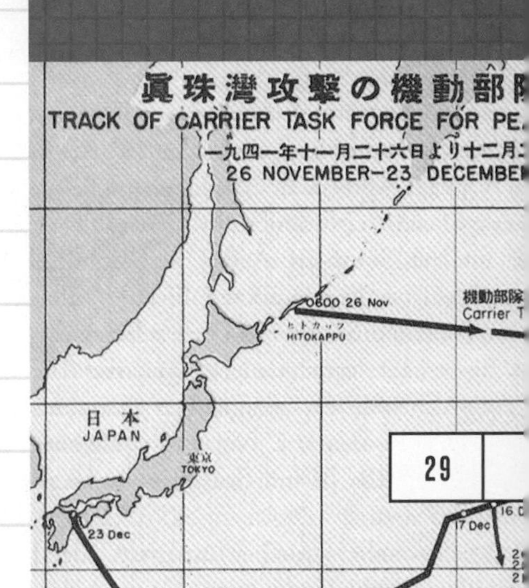

KHUKURI

With a reputation for deadly fighting prowess, Gurkha warriors were long associated with the khukuri (above), a knife with a curved blade, making it the perfect close-combat weapon. An Indian Army commander once stated famously: "If a man says he is not afraid of dying, he is either lying or he is a Gurkha."

NEPAL IN WWII

Nepalese soldiers, like those pictured on the left, fought in the British Gurkha units against the Axis all over the world. Gurkhas were part of the Allied occupation force in Japan.

Railroad, broad gauge, double track

10 LACHHIMAN GURUNG

BORN: 1917, CHITWAN, NEPAL

DIED: 2010, LONDON, ENGLAND

Lachhiman Gurung is known as the Gurkha (an indigenous soldier of Nepal) who kept 200 Japanese soldiers at bay in WWII. For his bravery, he was awarded the Victoria Cross, the highest and most prestigious British military honor.

He wasn't technically tall enough to enlist. But the British command needed every soldier for the raging conflict in Burma. Lachhiman was a rifleman in the 4th Battalion, 8th Gurkha Rifles, in the Indian Army. The year was 1945. Wounded in the forward-most trench on a hill, alone and outnumbered, he is said to have shouted at the enemy: "Come and fight a Gurkha!" He did this while firing a bolt-action rifle with his left hand. He had been using his right to lob enemy grenades right back at Japanese soldiers . . . until one exploded, blowing off fingers and breaking his arm.

With the help of wounded comrades, he held off every advance. Thirty-one dead enemy soldiers lay in the area before his trench. His valor inspired the platoon. For three days, they continued to repel, never losing ground, never losing hope. Lachhiman's heroic story appeared in British newspapers like the *London Gazette*, making him a legend.

He lost an eye and had his right hand amputated after three unsuccessful surgeries. But he stayed with the 8th Gurkhas until the war ended. In 1947, he returned to his village in Nepal and became a farmer. He was fitted with an artificial limb and lived to be 92 years old.

THE BURMA CAMPAIGN

It is called "the forgotten war." A four-year conflict in a challenging jungle environment (see photos above and below), it didn't offer a decisive outcome to WWII. As a result, Burma, which was a British colony during WWII, is often overlooked by journalists and historians.

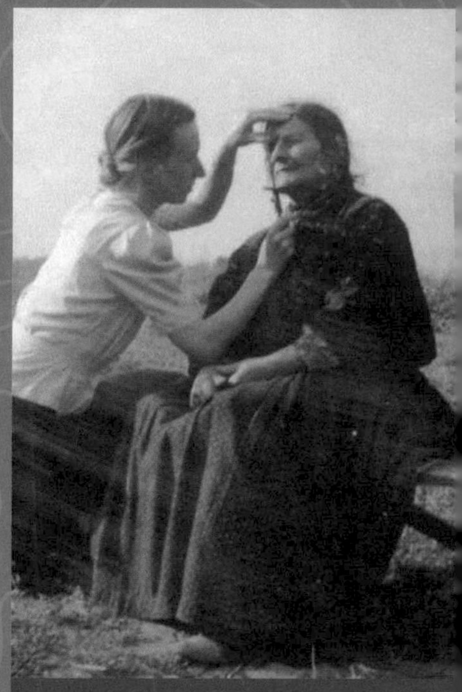

MASTER RACE

From the inception of the Nazi political party in the 1920s, Adolf Hitler and his followers embraced the concept of a superior race. They promoted the false belief in the existence of an "Aryan race" that was better than all others. Above and below, German researchers are photographed measuring features of racial minorities.

WHAT'S AN ARYAN?

European intellectuals in the 19th century used the term "Aryan" to classify the Indo-European or Indo-Germanic peoples who had settled in India, Persia (Iran), and Europe thousands of years ago. The classification described similarities among European languages, including Sanskrit and Persian (Farsi).

11

ABDOL HOSSEIN SARDARI

BORN: 1914, TEHRAN, IRAN
DIED: 1981, NOTTINGHAM, ENGLAND

He was dubbed "The Iranian Schindler" for saving thousands of Jews from the Holocaust. He was the best kind of hero at the worst moment in history. He risked his life to rescue others, making him an unforgettable savior and a symbol of selfless heroism.

Abdol Hossein Sardari was working as a diplomat in the Iranian consular office in Paris in 1942. There were many Iranian Jews in the city at the time. Nazis believed that Iranians were Aryan. Indeed, many scholars and historians had, in the years before WWII, elevated the idea of Aryans into a mythical and superior "race." This false concept was embraced by the Nazis. According to their racial theory, Nazis declared Iranians "pure-blooded Aryans" and therefore immune to persecution. Iranian Jews fell under this category, too, saving them from imprisonment and death.

Abdol began issuing passports to Iranian Jews and non-Iranian Jews. In other words, he gave 2,000 people, who were doomed to die, a way to escape Nazi-occupied France. He signed every single "valid" passport himself and refrained from stating the religion of the passport-holder.

Sadly, Abdol's life after the war was fraught with persecutions by other state forces. His wife, a Chinese opera singer, disappeared in China when she returned to ask her parents for their blessing to marry him. And he watched helplessly as the Iranian Revolution of 1979 resulted in the death of his nephew and the loss of all family possessions. He lived in England for the rest of his life.

TEHRAN CONFERENCE

This was a meeting that involved U.S. President Franklin Roosevelt and British Prime Minister Winston Churchill (both pictured above) and Soviet Premier Joseph Stalin in Tehran, Iran, from November 28 to December 1, 1943. The three world leaders coordinated their military strategy against the Nazis and the Empire of Japan.

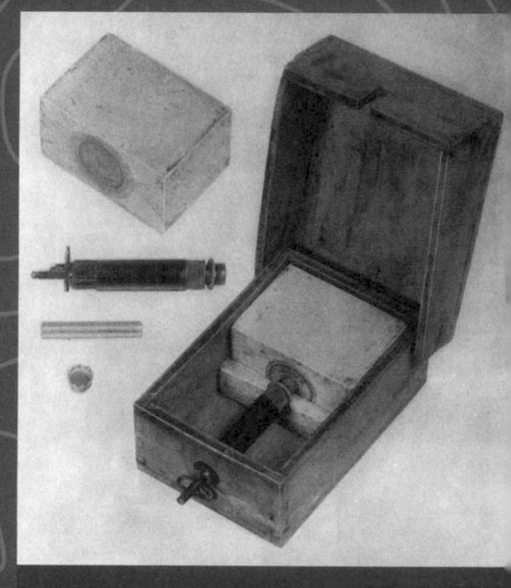

LAND MINES

According to a 1945 report by the U.S. Army, mines were responsible for 2.5 percent of combat fatalities and for 20.7 percent of tank losses across Europe. The German mine pictured above, the Schu-mine 42, was the most common mine used during the war.

CIVIL DEFENCE
WOMEN WANTED AS AMBULANCE DRIVERS

WOMEN DRIVERS

With men fighting on the front lines, American and British nurses were recruited for the dangerous task of driving ambulances (like in the British poster detail on the left). The role was challenging: Women had to endure the trauma of war while providing medical care in dangerous conditions, with the dead and wounded all around. Speed and safety were a necessity. On top of it all, nurses had to repair and maintain their own vehicles.

12 SUSAN TRAVERS

BORN: 1909, LONDON, ENGLAND
DIED: 2003, BALLAINVILLIERS, FRANCE

Her transition was unusual, moving from English socialite circles to sitting behind the wheel of a tank destroyer. It was even more surprising because she was a woman—the first and only female member of the French Foreign Legion.

The daughter of a Royal Navy admiral, Susan Travers grew up playing tennis and even competed at Wimbledon. When war broke out, she joined the French Red Cross as a nurse. But her appetite for adventure was insatiable, so she worked as an ambulance driver in Finland and as a chauffeur for a doctor in West Africa, Lebanon, and Syria. Eventually Susan met the colonel commanding the 1st Free French Division and became his driver.

During the Battle of Bir Hakeim in Libya in 1942, her navigation skills were put to the test. She led a convoy, retreating from German and Italian bombardment. The roof of her truck was ripped apart by a rocket shell, and she repaired it with the help of another driver. Susan dodged landmines and machine gun nests until she reached safety behind British lines. Upon examining her vehicle, the Allies saw that her car had a dozen bullet holes. The brakes were completely stripped.

She went on to serve in the Italian Campaign and the Western Front (France and Germany). Susan was wounded when her truck hit a mine. For her bravery, she earned the Legion of Honor, the highest French award bestowed upon miliary personnel and civilians.

When the war ended and her injuries healed, she applied to join the French Foreign Legion. By refusing to list her gender, her request was approved. She ended up as a driver with the legion during the First Indochina War. Susan married a fellow legionnaire and had two children. She waited until she was 91 to publish her account of WWII. It is called *Tomorrow to Be Brave: A Memoir of the Only Woman Ever to Serve in the French Foreign Legion.*

FEMALE NURSES ONLY

The nursing profession was limited to women during WWII. There was zero training for male nurses until well after the war. More than 350,000 women wore American service uniforms during WWII. Despite not serving in combat roles, 432 women died.

e Needed

GENEVA CONVENTIONS

The Geneva Conventions is a series of four international treaties created to protect noncombatants and prisoners of war during armed conflicts. The issue of weapons falls under the Hague Conventions (which cover conventional weapons), and the Geneva Protocol (biological and chemical attack). Above, leaders at the 1907 convention, including U.S. President Theodore Roosevelt, pose for a photograph.

D-DAY

The Normandy landings by Allied forces, pictured left, occurred on June 6, 1944. Often called D-Day or Operation Neptune, this was the largest seaborne invasion in history. This event marked the beginning of the liberation of France from the Nazis. D-Day sowed the seeds of Allied victory on the Western Front.

13 GUY STERN

BORN: 1922, HILDESHEIM, GERMANY
DIED: 2023, DETROIT, MICHIGAN

During WWII, he was a member of the Ritchie Boys, a U.S. military intelligence unit. Born in Germany, he spoke the language fluently. He conducted interrogations on the front line at D-Day.

Guy Stern's story is fascinating and bittersweet: At 15 years old, he was the only member of his immediate family to escape Nazi Germany. He made his way to St. Louis to live with his aunt and uncle during the tail end of the Great Depression. He did his best to secure safe passage for his parents and siblings, but his efforts were unsuccessful. His parents and siblings perished in the Holocaust. He didn't learn this until the war ended.

Guy was rejected by navy intelligence in 1942 for being German-born. A year later, he was drafted, then sent to Camp Ritchie in Maryland. There he was trained to use interrogation techniques. The Ritchie Boys strictly adhered to the Geneva Conventions, an established set of international legal standards for humanitarian treatment during war. Four nonviolent interrogation tactics Guy relied on were bribery, knowledge, shared interests, and fear.

With the help of another Ritchie Boy, Guy is credited with pioneering the "good cop, bad cop" approach, where one interrogator behaves threateningly while the other acts sympathetic. For the actionable intelligence he gathered during the Normandy Invasion, Guy received the Bronze Star.

After the war, he became a professor at Columbia University, where he taught literature. Guy was the director of the Harry and Wanda Zekelman International Institute of the Righteous at the Holocaust Memorial Center until his death at 101.

GREAT DEPRESSION

American prosperity in the 1920s collapsed with the stock market crash of 1929. The economic destruction of that period, referred to as the Great Depression, caused people to lose their jobs, bank accounts, and homes and farms. Only the massive, all-consuming mobilization for war with Japan and Germany finally cured the economic ills of the United States. Above, a destitute mother lives in a tent with her children. Below, crowds gather outside the Bank of the United States after it failed in 1931.

VETERANS AFFAIRS

The U.S. Department of Veterans Affairs (VA) is a branch department of the federal government tasked with providing lifelong healthcare services to military veterans. There are 170 VA medical centers and outpatient clinics all across the country. The VA also distributes benefits such as disability, vocational training, education assistance, home loans, and life insurance. The VA's present-day headquarters in Washington D.C. is pictured above.

G.I. BILL

In 1944, the G.I. Bill was signed into law by President Franklin D. Roosevelt to provide benefits to all WWII servicemen. These benefits included government payments made to veterans to cover the cost of tuition and living expenses to attend high school, college, or vocational school. On the left, a 1944 promotion poster depicts veterans attending college.

14 AUDIE MURPHY

BORN: 1925, KINGSTON, TEXAS
DIED: 1971, ROANOKE, VIRGINIA

Born into a Texas sharecropping family, Audie Murphy would become one of the most decorated combat soldiers of WWII. He would go on to become a film actor, starring in dozens of Western movies and TV episodes. A talented writer, his memoir, *To Hell and Back*, was adapted into a motion picture, in which he played himself. The songs he wrote would be recorded by the likes of Dean Martin.

Audie's sister helped him forge documents stating he was old enough to join the army. He fought in Italy and France and received every possible combat award for his actions. Most famously, at 19 years of age, he fended off an entire company of Nazis for an hour, then spearheaded a counterattack. What made this feat so incredible is that he did all this while wounded in both legs and while expending all of his rifle ammo on top of a burning vehicle. Audie received the Medal of Honor for his courage under fire.

His picture appeared on the cover of *Life* magazine in 1945, launching his film career. Audie prepared for his roles by rehearsing lines from the plays of William Shakespeare. He took up boxing and showcased his literary skills by writing books, song lyrics, poetry, and screenplays. He wept and expressed feelings of guilt whenever he happened to see news stories about German war orphans. Audie spoke up for veterans suffering from post-traumatic stress disorder. The Audie L. Murphy Memorial Veterans Affairs Hospital in San Antonio, Texas, opened in 1973, after his death in a plane crash.

CENTER FOR WOMEN VETERANS

Created in 1994, the Center for Women Veterans (CWA) is a branch of the Department of Veterans Affairs. Part of the CWA's stated mission is to raise awareness of the responsibility to treat women veterans with dignity and respect.

GESTAPO

Gestapo were the secret police of Nazi Germany. In German-occupied Europe, they hunted Jews, putting them in concentration camps. Above, Gestapo officers stationed in Czechoslovakia pose for a photograph.

GREECE DURING WWII

The Axis occupation of Greece during WWII began in April 1941 after the Germans and Italians invaded Greece. The occupation lasted until the Nazi withdrawal from the mainland in October 1944. To the left, German soldiers raise their flag over the ancient Acropolis in Athens.

15

PRINCESS ALICE OF BATTENBERG

BORN: 1885, WINDSOR CASTLE, ENGLAND
DIED: 1969, BUCKINGHAM PALACE, LONDON

The story goes that Princess Victoria Alice Elizabeth of Battenberg was born in the Tapestry Room in Windsor Castle. Though she was deaf, she learned to speak and lip-read English and German by the age of 8. She learned French and Greek as a young woman. She was diagnosed with schizophrenia and committed to sanitarium in Switzerland. Princess Alice is unlike any other royal figure in history.

She married Prince Andrew of Greece, living in Athens during WWII. Her two sons-in-law fought on the side the fascists, while her own son, Prince Philip, served in British Royal Navy. But Alice knew how evil Hitler was. She did everything she could to protect the persecuted.

Haimaki Cohen was a Jew and former member of the Greek Parliament. He sought refuge for his family but died on the run, leaving behind his widow, Rachel, and their children. As the Nazis arrived in Athens looking for Jews, Alice sheltered the Cohens in her home. It was a risky, remarkable act of kindness. The Cohens survived.

Deeply suspicious of Alice, the Gestapo stopped by several times. She used her deafness to pretend that she didn't understand German. Once a German officer knocked on her door, believing she supported the Nazi cause. "What can we do for you?" he said to her. She replied: "You can take your troops out of my country!"

Alice became religious and founded a nursing order of Greek Orthodox nuns. Following an episode of mental illness, she withdrew to a remote island. She returned to England and moved into Buckingham Palace to be with her son and grandchildren.

In 1993, years after her death, she was awarded the title of "Righteous Among the Nations" in Israel. in 2010, she was named "British Hero of the Holocaust" in England. She is buried in Gethsemane on the Mount of Olives in Jerusalem. Her son, Prince Phillip, said of her, "She was a person with deep religious faith and she would have considered it to be a totally human action to fellow human beings in distress."

GREEK JEWS

A total of 60,000 Greek Jews perished in the Holocaust. Thousands survived by going into hiding or by fighting alongside the partisans against the Nazis. Above, male Jews in Thessaloniki assemble for registration by the Nazis.

WHAT IS A CODE TALKER?

A "code talker" is the name given to Indigenous Americans who served in WWII. They used their tribal language to send secret communications on the battlefield, thereby thwarting Axis forces. Above, Comanche code talkers stand at Fort Gordon.

To the upper-left, Navajo code talkers in an artillery regiment in the South Pacific relay orders over a field radio in their native tongue. On the left, code talkers serving with the Marines operate a portable radio set in the jungle.

16 INDIGENOUS WARRIORS

The Navajo (Diné) code talkers had a secret weapon. Their traditional language was used to transmit Allied messages in the Pacific theater in WWII. However, at least 14 other Native nations (Cherokee, Comanche, and more) also served as code talkers.

In WWII, the U.S. military instituted a program to recruit and train Indigenous Americans to become code talkers. The irony of being asked to use their native tongue to fight for the United States instead of against the U.S. was not lost on these warriors. In fact, many had been forced to attend government or private Christian-run boarding schools. These schools worked hard to assimilate Native children. Punished for speaking their traditional language, they were now being asked to use it in order to defeat enemies abroad.

The Alaska Territorial Guard (ATG), also known as the Eskimo Scouts, was a military reserve force within the U.S. Army. Founded in 1942 in response to Pearl Harbor, the ATG operated until 1947.

More than 6,300 volunteers served without pay. They arrived from 107 different communities across Alaska. For the first time, different ethnic groups—Aleut, Athabaskan, White, Inupiaq, Haida, Tlingit, Tsimshian, Yupik, and others—combined forces. ATG served important roles as part of the Allied effort:

- They guarded the only source of the strategic metal platinum in the Western Hemisphere against Japanese attack.
- They secured the terrain near the air route between the United States and the Soviet Union.
- They placed and updated survival cachés along transportation corridors and coastal regions.

INDIGENOUS AMERICANS IN WWII

Approximately 44,000 Indigenous Americans served in WWII despite facing discrimination and being denied citizenship rights. Their contributions were diverse, spanning the Pacific and European theaters, like the 158th Infantry "Bushmasters" depicted above. Indeed, Native American servicemen and women played crucial roles, confounding enemy codebreakers and significantly enhancing Allied communications.

GREAT PATRIOTIC WAR

In Russia, all fighting on the Eastern Front during WWII is called the "Great Patriotic War." The battles waged in this theater comprised the largest, most death-dealing military clash in human history. It is estimated that 30 million people died fighting on the Eastern Front. A Russian war poster is shown above.

LUFTWAFFE

The Luftwaffe was the aerial-warfare branch of the Wehrmacht, the unified armed forces of Nazi Germany. These aviators played a huge role in German victories across Western Europe from 1939 to 1940. A great deal of Nazi aircraft production took place in concentration camps, with thousands of prisoners forced to manufacture planes and bombs. On the left, German Junkers fly over the Eastern Front.

17

VALENTINA GRIZODUBOVA

BORN: 1909, KHARVKIV, UKRAINE
DIED: 1993, MOSCOW, RUSSIA

She took her first flight at age 2. She was the first woman to earn the title of "Hero of the Soviet Union." In her twenties, she set several flying world records in distance, speed, and altitude. She led an aviation regiment, comprising more than 300 men, tasked with supplying partisans and bombing Nazi forces in southwestern Russia. Her name is Valentina Grizodubova, and this is her amazing story.

Her father, a renowned aircraft designer, shared his enthusiasm for flying with his daughter. At 14, she learned to pilot a glider by herself while studying piano at a music conservatory. At 20, Valentina graduated from a paramilitary flight school, impressing her teachers. She herself became an instructor, training dozens of male pilots who become decorated WWII aviation heroes.

In 1942, Valentina became the commander of the 101st Long-Range Aviation Regiment. Initially, male pilots scoffed, but she quickly earned their respect. She proved herself a skillful leader and combat strategist, performing 200 missions, including more than 100 night attacks. Anti-aircraft guns and the Luftwaffe tried to destroy her, but she persevered. The men began calling her "Mother," though she was only in her thirties. Her regiment ran 1,800 supply missions and evacuated 2,500 wounded partisans and war orphans out of Soviet-held areas along the Eastern Front. A fellow commander said of Valentina: "[She is] a very brave woman, decisive and daring in carrying out what was planned."

After the war, she helped train female cosmonauts to become test pilots. If you travel to Russia, you'll find a statue of Valentina in Moscow. You will also find streets named after her in cities all over the former Soviet territories.

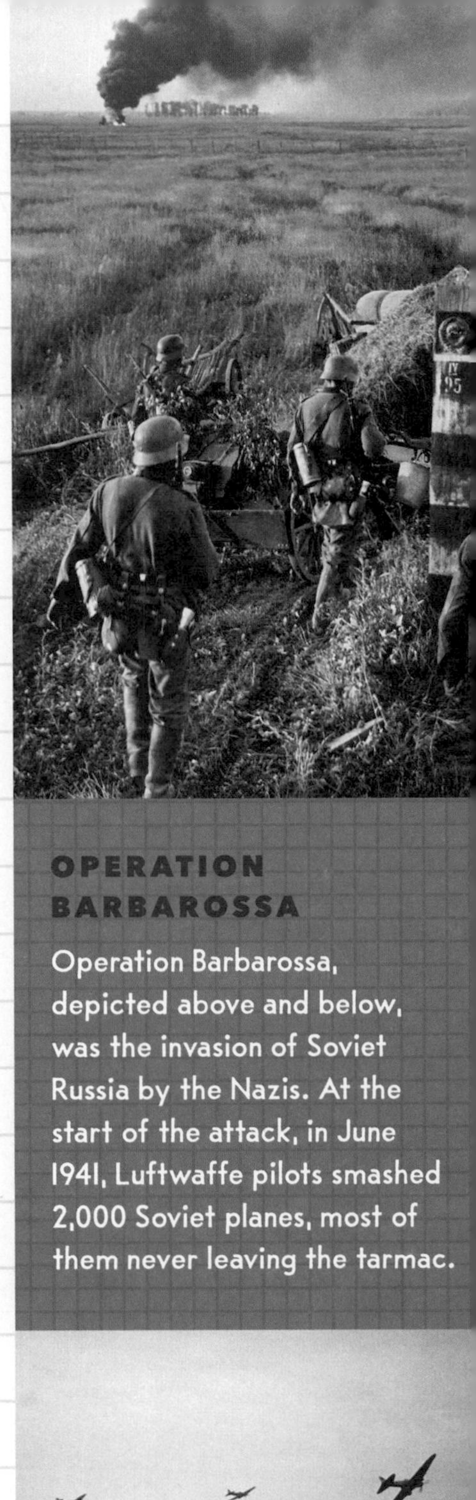

OPERATION BARBAROSSA

Operation Barbarossa, depicted above and below, was the invasion of Soviet Russia by the Nazis. At the start of the attack, in June 1941, Luftwaffe pilots smashed 2,000 Soviet planes, most of them never leaving the tarmac.

COMMONWEALTH GOVERNMENT

"Commonwealth" describes a political community that has been founded for the common good. The Commonwealth of the Philippines was a transitional government administration established in preparation for the country's independence. Before and during WWII, the United States managed the foreign affairs of the Philippines. Above, U.S. President Franklin D. Roosevelt stands with Commonwealth of the Philippines President Manuel L. Quezon.

PHILIPPINES DURING WWII

The Empire of Japan attacked the Philippines on December 8, 1941, nine hours after bombing Pearl Harbor. Although the Philippines was governed by a commonwealth government, the United States operated military bases there. To the left, Japanese tanks advance toward Manila.

18 JOSE CALUGAS

BORN: 1907, LEON, PHILIPPINES
DIED: 1998, TACOMA, WASHINGTON

Jose Calugas was raised to become a farmer. But with war on the horizon, he joined, at 23, a combat unit of Filipinos serving with U.S. forces. He was shipped to Camp Sill in Oklahoma, where he completed basic training, followed by artillery training. Learning to fire a heavy gun would come in handy.

Assigned to the 24th Field Artillery Regiment of the Philippine Scouts, Jose was posted at Fort Stotsenburg in the Philippines. He was on KP ("kitchen police") duty in the mess hall, when he noticed one of his unit's gun batteries had stopped firing. Jose dropped everything and ran 1,000 yards across a hostile landscape to reach the gun position. He instantly recruited a squad of fellow soldiers to put the weapon back in working order. They began returning fire, driving back Japanese forces. For this brave action, he became the first Filipino-American Medal of Honor recipient of WWII.

A month later, however, he was captured. Having survived the Bataan Death March, Jose suffered malnutrition and was beaten as a war prisoner for nearly a year. In January 1943, the Japanese put him to work in a rice mill. There he quietly joined a guerrilla unit, spying on the Japanese. Before too long, he escaped. Then he fought alongside another unit against the Japanese.

In 1957, Jose retired from the U.S. Army as a captain. He worked for Boeing, an aircraft design and manufacturing company in Tacoma, Washington.

TRAINING CHALLENGES

Language barriers complicated military training in the Philippines. Enlisted Filipinos, like those heralded in the war poster above, often spoke one language (Bikol or Visayan), while officers spoke another (Tagalog). Americans, meanwhile, only spoke English.

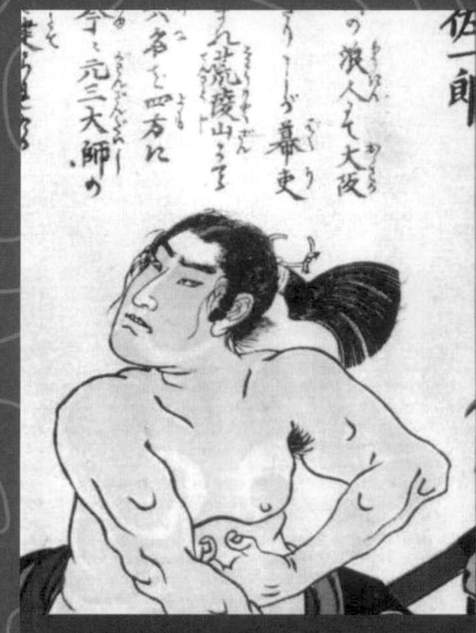

SEPPUKU

A form of ritual suicide originally practiced by Japan's samurai warriors, seppuku continued to be practiced by Japanese military leaders during WWII. Above, a Japanese woodblock print from the 1850s depicts the practice.

PUERTO RICO

The U.S. Department of Defense estimates that 65,000 Puerto Ricans, like those on the left, served in WWII. Most soldiers from the island served in the 65th Infantry Regiment and the Puerto Rico National Guard.

10

PEDRO AUGUSTO DEL VALLE

BORN: 1893, SAN JUAN, PUERTO RICO
DIED: 1978, ANNAPOLIS, MARYLAND

Born in Puerto Rico, back when the country was still controlled by Spain, Pedro del Valle moved to the United States as a child. He became the first Hispanic to reach the rank of lieutenant general. His career included service in WWI, through the U.S. occupation of Haiti (1915), and into WWII.

His entry into the Marines Corps was distinctive. The governor of Puerto Rico at the time appointed Pedro to attend the U.S. Naval Academy in Annapolis, Maryland. Pedro graduated from the academy in June 1915 and was commissioned a second lieutenant of the Marine Corps on June 5, 1915. While he always served with distinction, it was during WWII that his ferocious reputation was made.

Commanding the 11th Marine Regiment, Pedro led his men in the Guadalcanal Campaign. They provided artillery support for the 1st Marine Division in the Battle of the Tenaru. Pedro's gun units were relentless, decimating the Japanese onslaught before it reached Marine positions. Every enemy was killed. The defeat was so spectacular that a Japanese colonel committed seppuku out of shame.

Pedro was promoted to brigadier general and led the 3rd Corps Artillery in the Battle of Guam. Again, his heavy artillery performance was overwhelming, earning him a gold star. He again commanded his men brilliantly, this time commanding the 1st Marine Division, in the Battle of Okinawa. Pedro was awarded a Distinguished Service Medal for his leadership.

He is buried at the United States Naval Academy Cemetery and Columbarium.

FIELD ARTILLERY

Field artillery is mobile cannons and guns that are used to support attacking or defending armies in the field of battle. Above, the 240 mm howitzer M1 fires into German territory in Italy.

CARVE HER NAME WITH PRIDE

Violette Szabo's story was made into a 1956 book and then into a 1958 British film called *Carve Her Name with Pride.* Above, Violette's daughter, Tania, receives the George Cross award for bravery on her mother's behalf.

BRITISH SPECIAL OPERATIONS

During WWII, the British government's secret intelligence agency, Special Operations Executive (SOE), undermined Axis forces. SOE trained and deployed covert agents who infiltrated the Nazis to conduct reconnaissance, subversion, and sabotage. Thousands of SOE spies penetrated every theater of WWII—Poland, Ethiopia, Burma. But the organization's strongest presence was in France. To the left, agents-in-training take a demolitions class.

20

VIOLETTE SZABO

BORN: 1921, PARIS, FRANCE
DIED: 1945, RAVENSBRÜCK, GERMANY

There wasn't a braver, more beautiful agent of espionage than Violette Szabo. Four years before she died at age 24 in a concentration camp, she was a young perfume girl in London.

It was at a Bastille Day parade that Violette met dashing Etienne Szabo, an officer in the French Foreign Legion. They fell madly in love and married. But Etienne was soon dispatched to North Africa to fight the notorious Panzer tanks commanded by German General Rommel in the sands of Egypt. Violette's husband was killed in action, posthumously receiving the Croix de Guerre, the highest French military award for bravery. He never saw his daughter, born to Violette in London in the weeks before his death.

Heartbroken by her loss, Violette worked in an aircraft factory. She happened to meet a recruiter from British Special Operations. He observed that she was ideal spy material: athletic, French-speaking, and raised by a family comfortable around guns. She signed up for spy training and became an expert markswoman. Her parents would care for her daughter when she was in the field.

In 1944, after parachute and cryptography training, Violette was sent into France. Her mission: to sabotage German weapons factories. She was successful and excited to be making a difference. She was parachuted into France, this time just after D-Day to disrupt enemy communications. Paired with another spy, she encountered a roadblock and was forced to flee on foot. She exchanged gunfire, providing a distraction so that her partner could escape.

Captured by Nazis, Violette was imprisoned at Ravensbrück, a women's concentration camp, where many died. Violette was one of 40,000 victims, a hero to the end.

TALKING IN CODE

Cryptography and cryptoanalysis, the study and then "breaking" of coded communications, were practiced extensively in World WWII because of radio communication and the ease of eavesdropping. A major codebreaking event during the war was the Allied decryption of Nazi "Enigma" code.

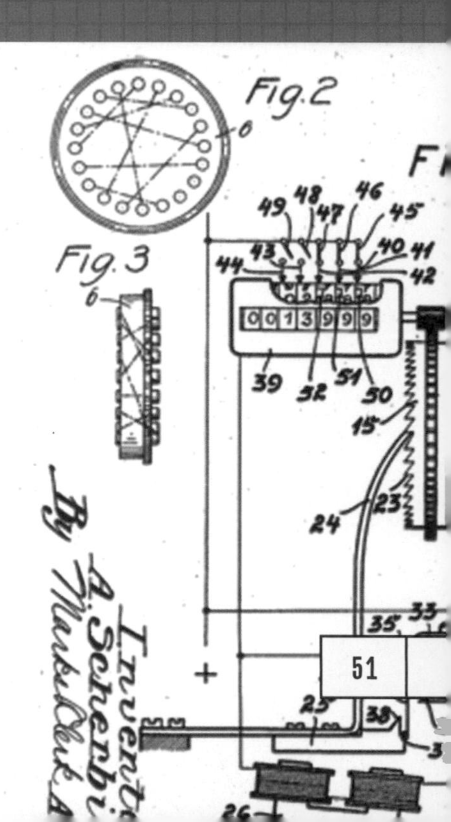

SOCIAL DOCUMENTARIANS

During WWII, most photographers believed in the American cause for defeating the Axis. A great number of these war photographers emerged from the 1930s tradition of social documentary photography, which captures what the world really looks like, with a social/environmental focus. Above, a Canadian photographer at sea holds a Fairchild K-20 camera.

CAMERA TECHNOLOGY

Unlike the First World War, photographs taken during WWII could be transmitted across oceans and continents. Airplanes could quickly drop or deliver rolls of film. The introduction of the telephoto lenses was also a significant advancement. To the left, a British photographer uses his Super Ikonta camera while in a trench in Northern Africa.

21 W. EUGENE SMITH

BORN: 1918, WICHITA, KANSAS
DIED: 1978, TUCSON, ARIZONA

He was a journalist who snapped photos on the frontlines in the Pacific theater. He was there when Allied forces unleashed an island-hopping offensive. He captured it all: savage violence, brutal agony, and human compassion. He photographed U.S. Marines and Japanese prisoners at Saipan, Guam, Iwo Jima, and Okinawa. Though he wasn't a pacifist, W. Eugene Smith mourned the consequences of war.

He launched his career at age 15, doing professional photo assignments for two Kansas newspapers. He studied at the New York City Institute of Photography for a year, before working as a photographer at *Newsweek* magazine.

One of Eugene's most memorable images is *A Japanese freighter in Truk Atoll is hit by a torpedo dropped by a U.S. aeroplane*, originally published in a 1944 issue of *Popular Photography*. Another iconic image of WWII: *Alert Soldier, Saipan*, featuring Angelo Klonis, a Greek immigrant who enlisted to secure U.S. citizenship.

Eugene is famously quoted as saying, "I want my pictures to carry some message against the greed, the stupidity, and the intolerances that cause these wars and the breaking of many bodies." After publishing his work in magazines like *Life*, Eugene was wounded while photographing the Battle of Okinawa.

When the war ended, Eugene joined Magnum Photos, an international image cooperative. He found success there but developed a reputation for being "difficult" due to his principles and aesthetic. He took photos for a project called Minamata, which documented the effects of industrial mercury poisoning in the Japanese city of Minamata.

Today there is a W. Eugene Smith Fund, which awards photographers for their exceptional accomplishments in the artform.

SO MANY PICTURES

U.S. Armed Forces had their own teams of picture-takers. Military combat photographers supplied over a half million still pictures to the U.S. and British media. Above, General MacArthur returns with U.S. forces to the Philippines. Below, navy mechanics work in Texas.

TREBLINKA

Built and operated by Nazis in occupied Poland during WWII, Treblinka was an extermination camp in the forest outside of Warsaw. During the deadliest phase of the Final Solution, 900,000 Jews died in its gas chamber. Above, Polish Jews are forced onto trains that will take them to Treblinka.

WARSAW UPRISING

This was an effort by the Polish underground to liberate Warsaw from the Nazis. It happened in the summer of 1944. The uprising coincided intentionally with the Nazi retreat ahead of the Soviet advance. To the left, Polish partisans drive a German armored vehicle they've captured.

22

IRENA SENDLER

BORN: 1910, WARSAW, POLAND
DIED: 2008, WARSAW, POLAND

As a 29-year-old social worker in Nazi-occupied Poland, Irena Sendler felt powerless. But she used her job, helping the poor and vulnerable in society, to assist and protect Jews. With Gestapo unleashed in Poland, time was running out. Many Jewish people were being thrown into camps.

Irene grew up without prejudicial feelings toward Jews. Her husband, a Polish soldier, was captured during the Nazi invasion of Poland. This gave Irene reason to resist German occupation. In her role, she began fabricating medical documents for the Jewish community. This allowed Jews to find care in spite of German prohibitions. Irene also visited the dreaded, disease-ridden Warsaw Ghetto, where Nazis had sealed off most Polish Jews. Pretending to conduct sanitary inspections, she instead brought medicine, cleaning supplies, fresh clothing, and food. She helped smuggle Jews out of the ghetto and secure safe housing for them.

But the Holocaust was well underway. The Nazis transported Warsaw Ghetto inhabitants to an extermination camp called Treblinka. Irene and others formed the Council for Aid to Jews. This organization cared for thousands of Jews in hiding, keeping them safe. When the Warsaw Ghetto was destroyed in 1943, Irene arranged with orphanages and institutes for abandoned children to have Jewish children sent there. She was arrested for helping Jews and sentenced for execution. But bribes from friends spared her, and she was able to hide. Irene joined the Warsaw Uprising, working as a field nurse until the Nazis fled.

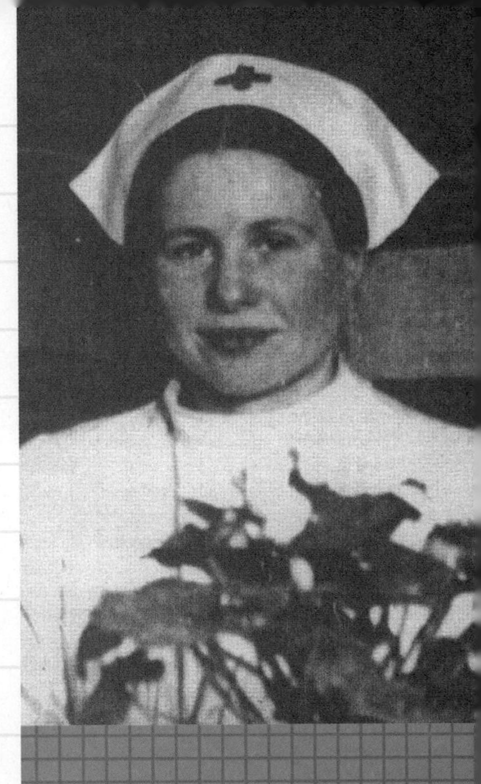

LIFE IN A JAR

Before 1999, the name Irene Sendler meant little in the United States until a Kansas schoolteacher encouraged his students to learn about the Holocaust. Together they discovered the story of a brave woman in Poland (pictured above), mentioned only briefly in a magazine. The teacher produced a successful play based on his students' research called *Life in a Jar*.

ON BEHALF OF THE CROWN

India deployed 2.5 million soldiers, like those left and above, to fight under British command against the Axis. They were valiant fighters who fought in the European theater against Germany, in the North African campaign against fascist Italy, and in the Southeast Asian theater. Soldiers from India also defended the Indian subcontinent against Japanese forces.

YESHWANT GHADGE

Yeshwant Ghadge, shown left, was 22 years old when he fought with the 5th Mahratta Light Infantry in Italy. Under heavy fire, with many of his comrades killed, Yeshwant grabbed a machine gun while tossing a grenade to discourage a charge. He picked off the remaining fascists. Still, two more soldiers advanced. With no time to reload, he used the butt of his rifle to neutralize them However, a sniper, unseen at a distance, shot Yeshwant dead.

23 SOLDIERS FROM INDIA

Some of the bravest soldiers to fight for the Queen against the Axis menace were Indians.

RAO ABDUL HAFIZ KHAN

Rao Abdul Hafiz Khan, left, was only 18 years old he when he served in the British Indian Army in the 9th Jat Regiment (infantry). He fought at the Battle of Imphal in April 1944. Abdul led his platoon across a bare slope that reached a steep hill. Japanese soldiers fired their guns and used grenades, the blasts injuring Abdul. He continued to climb. Upon reaching the enemy bunker, he wrested a machine gun from a soldier with his bare hands and pushed his platoon onward. Abdul died from his wounds, even as he continued to return fire.

FAZAL DIN

Fazal Din, illustrated above, was 23 years old in the 7th Battalion, 10th Baluch Regiment. Surrounded by three bunkers, Fazal tossed a grenade at the bunker closest to him, wrecking it. Against heavy fire, he pushed his troops ahead. Face-to-face with Japanese soldiers, he didn't retreat. A soldier ran him through with a sword, but Fazal yanked the blade from his own body and hacked the soldier, killing him. With a giant wound in his body, he killed more enemy soldiers before succumbing himself.

USS *OKLAHOMA*

In the Japanese attack on Pearl Harbor, torpedo bombers struck the ship, causing it to capsize, as photographed above. More than 400 crewmen died. Survivors jumped from a height of 50 feet into boiling water or climbed across mooring lines that connected the *Oklahoma* and USS *Maryland*. Others escaped when rescuers drilled holes into the burning ship to drag them out.

PEARL HARBOR NATIONAL MEMORIAL

Located on the island of Oahu in Hawaii, the Pearl Harbor National Memorial, left, commemorates the attack on Pearl Harbor. More than 2,400 Americans died and twelve ships sank.

24

JULIUS ELLSBERRY

BORN: 1921, BIRMINGHAM, ALABAMA
DIED: 1941, PEARL HARBOR, HAWAII

Julius Ellsberry was a young American killed during the Japanese bombing of Pearl Harbor on December 7, 1941. He was the first person from Alabama to die in WWII and among the first Americans killed in the Pacific theater. But he died in an effort to rescue others and is today honored as a hero.

Born in Birmingham, Alabama, Julius graduated from Parker High School in 1938. He enlisted in the U.S. Navy two years later. He had wanted to join the service before his 18th birthday, but it would require his parents to sign forms and documents. He decided to wait.

The U.S. Armed Forces were segregated when Ellsberry joined the Navy. He was one of only 62 African-Americans in the entire Pacific fleet.

With a rank of mess attendant first class, he was aboard the USS Oklahoma when Japanese planes bombed Pearl Harbor in a surprise attack. He and 400 other crewmen were killed. He was awarded a posthumous Purple Heart in honor of his sacrifice.

The Black community in his hometown of Birmingham raised $300,000 in war-bond purchases. (This is the equivalent of $4 million today.) The money went toward the construction of a B-24 Liberator bomber plane, also known as *The Spirit of Ellsberry*.

Ellsberry Park, north of downtown Birmingham, was dedicated in his honor in 1979.

WAR BONDS

War bonds were issued by the U.S. government to finance military operations during WWII. Bonds helped prevent a tax increase. They also curbed inflation by removing money from circulation in a wartime economy. The government used posters like those above and below to encourage citizens to purchase bonds.

7.50	390.00	2,009.02	4,329

NO RESPECT

The all-female aviation regiment of Night Witches wasn't always welcome. Many male pilots saw them as inferior. The witches were given thirdhand uniforms and bulky shoes, as well as shoddy gear. Nevertheless, what the Night Witches achieved was incredible. Irina Sebrova, photographed above, flew over 1,000 sorties herself!

SOVIET AIR FORCE

The Soviets produced 157,000 aircraft during the Great Patriotic War (WWII). More than 125,655 of these were designed for combat. The Lavochkin La-5, illustrated on the left, had over 9,000 units built alone.

25 NADEZHDA POPOVA

BORN: 1921, SHABANOVKA, RUSSIA
DIED: 2013, MOSCOW, RUSSIA

Nadezhda Popova was a squadron commander in the legendary Soviet Night Bomber Regiment, also called the Night Witches. After her brother was killed fighting Nazis and her family home was seized, she exacted revenge by flying 800-plus bombing and reconnaissance missions against the Wehrmacht. She is among the most highly decorated warriors of WWII.

Nadezhda grew up in the coal fields in Ukraine. She was a wild teenager who loved music and dancing. Once, she observed a small plane land near her village. That was it: She was hooked. Without letting her parents know, she enrolled in gliding school at 15. This simple act of rebellion would put her on a path to heroism.

A year later, she made her first parachute jump and solo flight. She was accepted into flight school, graduating and becoming an instructor at 18. She was recruited into the Night Witches, tasked with bombing raids on enemy ammo dumps, convoys, and troops. The regiment's name came from their unusual craft and tactics: In wooden-and-canvas biplanes designed for crop-dusting, pilots would idle their engines and glide over targets to drop their firebombs. The Germans heard the whooshing of these otherwise loud planes; it sounded like the broomsticks of witches flying in darkness.

Nadezhda was shot down several times but never badly wounded. She was on reconnaissance mission when Luftwaffe fighters forced her to crash-land. In search of her unit, she joined a retreating column of wounded Soviet infantrymen. Among them, she met her future husband, a fighter pilot. They married after the war.

NUMBERS

The Night Witches accumulated 28,676 flight hours, dropped 3,000 tons of bombs and 26,000 firebombs, destroying river crossings, railways, warehouses, fuel depots, armored vehicles, and searchlights.

WORKS CITED

"Abdolhossein Sardari: An Iranian Hero of the Holocaust." United States Holocaust Memorial Museum. Retrieved March 23, 2023.

Anthonioz, Geneviève de Gaulle. *The Dawn of Hope: A Memoir of Ravensbrück*. New York: Arcade Publishers, 1999.

Atwood, Kathyrn J. "Irena Sendler." *Woman Heroes of World War II*. Chicago: Chicago Review, 2011. 43–48.

Barkawi, Tarak. "Culture and Combat in the Colonies: The Indian Army in the Second World War." *Journal of Contemporary History* 41, no. 2 (2006): 325–55. JSTOR, http://www.jstor.org/stable/30036389. Accessed March 30, 2023.

Barrett, Claire. "Guy Stern: War of Words." HistoryNet, August 27, 2020. https://www.historynet.com/guy-stern-war-of-words/. Accessed March 30, 2023.

Beers, Carole (January 24, 1998). "Jose Calugas, Medal of Honor Winner, Death March Survivor." *Seattle Times*. Retrieved May 22, 2009. Accessed March 30, 2023.

Bevans, Charles I., comp. *Treaties and Other International Agreements of the United States of America, 1776–1949* 2, page 43 (electronic copy from HathiTrust). https://guides.loc.gov/treaty-of-versailles.

Cook, K. (2020). "The Indian Who Raised the Flag: An Examination of the Legacy of Ira Hayes, 1945–Present" (Order No. 28151006). Available from ProQuest One Academic; Publicly Available Content Database. (2455588915). Retrieved from https://www.ezproxy.library.unlv.edu/login?url=https://www.proquest.com/dissertations-theses/indian-who-raised-flag-examination-legacy-ira/docview/2455588915/se-2.

Cottam, Kazimiera J. "Soviet Women Soldiers in World War II: Three Biographical Sketches." *Minerva: Quarterly Report on Women and the Military*, fall–winter 2000, p. 16. Gale Academic OneFile, link.gale.com/apps/doc/A73063465/AONE?u=anon~-80ca530b&sid=googleScholar&xid=4434bd9c. Accessed March 30, 2023.

Danner, Dorothy Still. *What a Way to Spend a War: Navy Nurse POWs in the Philippines*. Annapolis, MD: Naval Institute Press, 1995.

Del Valle, Pedro Augusto. *Semper Fidelis: An Autobiography*. Hawthorne, CA: Christian Book Club of America, 1976.

Dell, Pamela. *The Soviet Night Witches: Brave Women Bomber Pilots of World War II*. North Mankato, MN: Capstone Press, 2018.

Donovan, Robert J. *PT 109: John F. Kennedy in World War II*. 40th anniversary ed. New York: McGraw-Hill, 2001.

Doss, Frances M. *Desmond Doss: Conscientious Objector; The Story of an Unlikely Hero*. Nampa, Ont.: Pacific Press Pub. Association, 2005.

Foss, Joe, and Donna Wild Foss. *A Proud American: The Autobiography of Joe Foss.* New York: Pocket Books, 1992.

Gilbert, Martin. "Salute those unsung heroes of the Holocaust." *The Guardian*, January 21, 2006. http://www.guardian.co.uk/world/2006/jan/22/secondworldwar.comment. Retrieved March 30, 2023.

Haugen, David M., and Susan Musser. *The Attack On Pearl Harbor*. Detroit: Greenhaven Press, 2011.

Hendricks, Charles. "The Eskimos and the Defense of Alaska." *Pacific Historical Review* 54, no. 3 (1985): 271–95. JSTOR, https://doi.org/10.2307/3639633. Accessed March 30, 2023.

Kobre, Ken. "Last Interview with W. Eugene Smith on the Photo Essay" [microform] / Ken Kobre Distributed by ERIC Clearinghouse [Washington, D.C.] 1979.

Kramer, R. Violette Szabo. *The Journal of Military History* 67, no. 1 (2003): 268–69. Retrieved from https://www.ezproxy.library.unlv.edu/login?url=https://www.proquest.com/scholarly-journals/violette-szabo/docview/195628069/se-2.

Leff, Mark. "The Politics of Sacrifice on the American Home Front in World War II," *Journal of American History* 77 (March 1991): 1296–318.

Lichtenstein, Nelson. *Labor's War at Home: The CIO in World War II*. Philadelphia: Temple University Press, 2003, 82–109.

Murphy, Audie. *To Hell and Back.* New York: H. Holt, 1949.

Nobus, D. "The madness of Princess Alice: Sigmund Freud, Ernst Simmel and Alice of Battenberg at Kurhaus Schloß Tegel." *History of Psychiatry* 31, no. 2 (2020):147–62. doi:10.1177/0957154X19898597.

Saidel, Rochelle G. *The Jewish Women of Ravensbrück Concentration Camp*. Madison, WI: University of Wisconsin Press, 2004.

Southern Kentucky Festival of Books. "The A-Train: Memoirs of a Tuskegee Airman." C-Span Video Library. Video file, 54:43. April 12, 2003. Accessed March 25, 2023. https://www.c-span.org/video/?176374-6/the-train-memoirs-tuskegee-airman.

Smith, W. Eugene, and Robert L. Kirschenbaum. *W. Eugene Smith*. [Japan], PPS, 1982.

Steinberg, David Joel. *Philippine Collaboration in World War II.* Ann Arbor: University of Michigan Press, 1967.

Tahmahkera, Dustin. "An Indian in a White Man's Camp': Johnny Cash's Indian Country Music." *American Quarterly* 63, no. 3 (2011): 591–617. JSTOR, http://www.jstor.org/stable/41237568. Accessed March 30, 2023.

Wundheiler, Luitgard N. "Oskar Schindler's Moral Development During the Holocaust." *Humboldt Journal of Social Relations* 13, 1–2 (1986): 333–56. JSTOR, http://www.jstor.org/stable/23262673. Accessed March 30, 2023.

About the Author

Jarret Keene is an assistant professor in the English department at the University of Nevada, Las Vegas, where he teaches American literature and the graphic novel. He has written books (travel guide, rock-band biography, poetry collections) and edited short-fiction anthologies. His YA dystopian novel *Hammer of the Dogs* has been featured in *Writer's Digest* and *Publishers Weekly*. His books for Bushel & Peck Books include *Heroes of World War II* and *Decide & Survive: Attack on Pearl Harbor*.

About the Illustrator

Ricardo Gualberto is an artist based in Brazil. His bold colors and simple shapes adorn numerous publications.

About Bushel & Peck Books

Bushel & Peck Books is a children's publishing house with a special mission. Through our Book-for-Book Promise™, we donate one book to kids in need for every book we sell. Our beautiful books are given to kids through schools, libraries, local neighborhoods, shelters, nonprofits, and also to many selfless organizations who are working hard to make a difference. So thank you for purchasing this book! Because of you, another book will find its way into the hands of a child who needs it most.

Our Giving

We can't solve every problem in the world, but we believe children's books can help. Illiteracy is linked to many of the world's greatest challenges, including crime, school dropout rates, and drug use. Yet impressively, just the presence of books in a home can be a leg up for struggling kids. Unfortunately, many children in need find themselves without adequate access to age-appropriate books. One study found that low-income neighborhoods have, in some US cities, only one book for every three hundred kids (compared to thirteen books for every one child in middle-income neighborhoods). With our Book-for-Book Promise™, Bushel & Peck Books is putting quality children's books into the hands of as many kids as possible. We hope these books bring an increased interest in reading and learning, and with that, a greater chance for future success. To learn more about how we give, including our annual Giving Plan and commitment to carbon-neutral shipments, or to nominate a school or organization to receive free books, please visit bushelandpeckbooks.com.